THE BODY
Sacrament

written by
A. W. Mausolf

illustrated by
Jennifer Soriano

Level 5
BOOK 1

TOBET **THEOLOGY OF THE BODY EVANGELIZATION TEAM**

Dedicated to the Church, including our family and friends,
and especially to Mother Mary and Saint John Paul.

Tremendous thanks to all TOBET members over the years.
Special thanks to Andrea, Joanna, Kathy, Sarah, Tamara, and Véronique.

We are grateful for consultation work by the translator of the Theology of the Body,
Dr. Michael Waldstein, as well as Dr. Susan Waldstein and Dr. Danielle M. Peters.

Nihil Obstat: David Uebbing, B.A., M.A.
                  Censor Librorum

Imprimatur: +Most Reverend Samuel J. Aquila, S.T.L.
                Archbishop of Denver
                Denver, Colorado, USA
                October 16, 2017

Library of Congress information on file. ISBN 978-1-945845-51-2

Cover Design: FigDesign • Layout: Emily Gudde • Editor: Dayspring Brock • Associate Editor: Alexis Mausolf

Excerpts from the English translation of the *Catechism of the Catholic Church*. New York: Catholic Book Publishing Co., 1994.

Based on *Man and Woman He Created Them: A Theology of the Body* translated by Michael Waldstein, Copyright © 2006. Used by permission of Pauline Books & Media, 50 Saint Paul's Ave, Boston, Massachusetts 02130. All rights reserved. www.pauline.org.

John Paul II. "Redemptor Hominis." *The Holy See*, March 4, 1979, para. 10, w2.vatican.va

All Scripture verses are from the *New American Bible*, Revised Edition (NABRE).

Excerpt from *YOUCAT*. Trans. Michael J. Miller. (San Francisco: Ignatius Press, 2011), www.ignatius.com. Used with permission.

Table of Contents

1 The Sacraments

Mother Church

Did you know that the Church is our Mother?
We are her children.

Are you thinking, *"What? I have another mother, and it's a building?"*

No, not the building. We also call
the group of people inside our church
buildings "the Church." You see, just as a
good mother gives life to her children and
gives them good things to help them be happy,
so Mother Church gives us good things that bring
us life and happiness. Some of these are the Sacraments.
Think about the Sacraments for a moment.

4

Imagine Mother Church embracing you, a new child, kissing you on the forehead, bringing you into the family circle, nourishing you, and helping you grow to adulthood. She does this with **Baptism**, **Confirmation**, and the **Eucharist**.

If we are hurt or sick in soul or body, Mother Church tends to us with the Sacraments of **Reconciliation** and **Anointing of the Sick.**

The Church unites us to other people and can send us forth to help build God's kingdom on earth with the Sacraments of **Matrimony** and **Holy Orders.** There is a lot of love in each of these Sacraments.

Look at this chart to compare how you grow in each stage of your life.

Human Life		Life in God
(in my Family)		**(in the Sacraments)**
Birth—Receiving my Life		**Baptism**—Receiving God's Life in Me
Growth—Strength in Body & Spirit to Serve Others		**Confirmation**—Strength from God to Serve Others
Nourishment—Food & Drink for Body		**Eucharist**—Food & Drink for Soul
Medicine—For Bodily Illness		**Reconciliation**—For Spiritual Illness (Sin)
Marriage—Building the Family		**Matrimony**—Building the Church
Fatherhood—Natural Life & Guidance		**Priesthood**—Spiritual Life & Guidance
Suffering & Death—End of Life		**Anointing of the Sick**—Preparation for New Life

What Is a Sacrament?

A Sacrament is **a visible sign that brings about an invisible reality**. Sacraments are always both visible and invisible. What we see with our eyes is not the whole picture.

When participating in the Sacraments, we can know that something invisible is happening. You see, Sacraments are not **just** signs. They are signs that have power, the power to change us and to change reality. Why? In every Sacrament, we meet a Person—a powerful, divine Person. We meet Jesus Christ.

A sacrament is a visible sign of an invisible reality, and in this sign — God gives himself to man.

Theology of the Body 87:5

Invisible but Real

You might say, *"Wait a minute! What is an invisible reality? Are invisible things even real?"*

Why yes! Just because we cannot SEE something doesn't mean it is not real. We cannot SEE gravity, but we know it's there when we accidentally drop a glass and see it fall and break!

We don't know what brain waves look like, but doctors know they exist. You cannot SEE the thoughts of your friends, but you know by their words and bodily actions that they are thinking. We cannot SEE angels or Wi-Fi connections or music or electricity. All of these things are invisible. We cannot SEE the smell of fresh-baked bread, or SEE the sound of waves crashing on the beach. What else is invisible? Truth is invisible, fear is invisible, hunger is invisible. Yet all are real!

Can you name some other invisible realities?

We can also name lots of visible things like soccer balls, candy, and new shoes. Both visible and invisible things exist, but that does not mean that they have the power to change us and reality like a Sacrament does. You could have a pretend Mass at home, but you don't have the power to change the bread into the Body of Christ!

Sacraments Have Power

Sacraments are both visible and invisible AND have power. What we see, hear, smell, taste, and touch in the Sacraments points to the invisible way God is working in our souls. His presence gives the Sacraments their power and their effectiveness. In the Sacraments, we **meet** Christ.

Pretend you are putting on a special pair of glasses that give you enhanced vision. With these glasses you see not only the surfaces of things but their hidden realities too. We could call these our sacramental "Son-glasses." Put on those imaginary glasses, and let's focus on two very important Sacraments now to see how we can meet God in both.

Baptism is the Sacrament of mission and the foundation of all other sacraments where we encounter Christ. Through Baptism we are born into the family of God. Just as your earthly mom gave **birth** to you, Mother Church gave **rebirth** to you in Baptism.

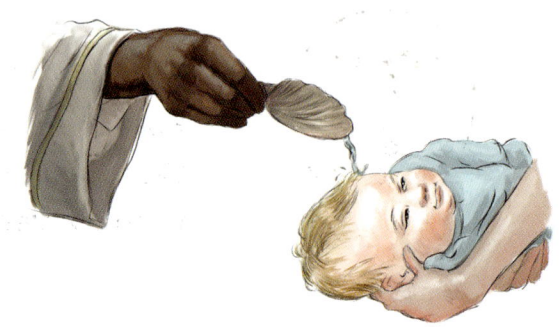

Baptism

 **Visible**

Invisible 👓

When the priest poured holy water on your forehead...	... God really and truly washed you clean from the stain of original sin. Water is used for washing and for cleaning.
When the priest anointed your head with a sweet-scented oil called chrism...	... God anointed you: He chose you and set you apart to serve others. The sweet smell means you are pleasing to God!
When the priest said, "I baptize you in the name of the Father and of the Son and of the Holy Spirit..."	... God shared with you His own DIVINE life! You became a member of God's family, the Church.

10

The Church feeds our bodies and souls with the Body of Christ, the Sacrament of the Eucharist. We approach the altar, knowing that we are about to receive **Jesus' Body** within **our own bodies!**

Eucharist

 **Visible**
                Invisible

Visible	Invisible
When we hear the priest repeat the words of Our Lord at the Last Supper, "This is my Body…"	… God transforms the bread and wine into the Body and Blood of Jesus!
When the priest elevates (lifts up or offers) Jesus' Body and Blood…	… the Son offers Himself to the Father in the power of the Holy Spirit. The Trinity is present with us.
When we approach the altar, receive the Eucharist, and consume the Body of Christ…	… Christ enters our bodies with His Body. He is united with us as one spiritual body. We can freely open ourselves to God. We are a gift to Him, and He is a gift to us, His Body, Blood, Soul, and Divinity.

The Body and the Sacraments

"Why are we talking about the Sacraments in a book about my body?" Because all of the Sacraments have to do with the body!

We meet Christ
in every Sacrament!

"Why do all of the Sacraments have to do with the body?" Because Jesus Christ wants us to experience God's action through our bodies in order to show us what is happening in our whole selves.

God made our bodies and they are good. God also made all of matter, which is also good. We need bodies AND matter to receive the Sacraments.

We use baptismal waters for washing, Eucharistic Bread for eating, holy oils for anointing, and so on. You can examine the Sacraments to find what we sense with our bodies AND how we meet God invisibly in each one.

God can meet us however He wants and whenever He wants, but in these seven Sacraments, we know what God is doing and when. What a gift!

"All Sacraments are an encounter with Christ, who is himself the original sacrament." *YOUCAT 193*

Mission: The next time you receive the Eucharist, whisper quietly, "Nice to meet You again in this Sacrament, Jesus!"

2 The Body as a Sacrament

Hidden Realities

Look at these emojis! What is each one trying to tell us? What invisible reality does each image hide? The pictures make us smile, but they also convey special meanings.

There are many things that we cannot see with our eyes, but they are real and true nevertheless.

In our last lesson, we saw that there can be hidden realities behind the things around us.

What Is a Symbol?

Symbols are like sacraments, but they are not the same thing. Can you think of examples when a deeper meaning is hiding behind something you see?

For example, when you see written sheet music, you don't just think it is a page of interesting scribbles; you know it represents a series of musical sounds. It might even remind you of a violinist.

We learn to connect many common invisible realities to certain pictures or objects, so that we can "see" them in our minds. These pictures and objects are **symbols**.

 Do you know what a white flag symbolizes?

 What does a heart symbolize?

 What do a skull and crossbones symbolize?

 Does a lion make you think of kingship and power?

 Does the sun remind you of God's light and warm presence?

Some symbols are more personal and only have meaning for you. When you look at your school backpack, you don't just think of its size and color, but what it represents: hard work and your life at school. You might see your mother's perfume bottle as a symbol. It represents her beauty.

Maybe you see your father's toolbox as a symbol. It could represent how hard he works for your family and provides for you. Do you remember playing with a favorite toy when you were much smaller? That toy can be a symbol, and it represents your childhood!

Symbols have invisible meanings, but they have no power to change reality. Sacraments do! Sacraments show visibly what they work invisibly.

What if a common symbol were to become like a sacrament? Picture a normal stop sign. It is a symbol of traffic laws. The sign warns us to stop, but it has no real power to make that happen. What if you were driving along and the stop sign suddenly jumped out in front of your car and made it stop? Then, that stop sign would be like a sacrament!

The Body as Sacrament

What about your body? Is it only a symbol, or is it like a sacrament? Does your body represent you, like a symbol, or IS it you? Think about the body. Your body is a visible sign that brings about invisible realities. Through your body, you make visible what you're thinking, deciding, feeling, and loving.

This is what Saint John Paul tells us:

"**The body... and only the body, is capable of making visible what is invisible: the spiritual and the divine.**"

Theology of the Body 19:4

"What does it mean when we say that the body is like a sacrament?"

It means that the visible body brings about some invisible realities. The body can reveal the spirit, the mind, the imagination. With the invisible parts of us we plan, hope, love, choose, and remember.

Because we are made of things seen and unseen, our bodies are signs of us as "whole people." Body and spirit belong together and make us who we are.

A whole human person is body and spirit together. A body and spirit that are separated means that the person is not alive, but dead. In heaven, our perfected spirits and our perfected bodies will be joined again!

Not Angel... Not Animal... But Human!

In the beginning, God made the angels as spiritual beings. He made animals with a mortal soul animating the animal body.

God did something different when He created humans, though. He gave Adam and Eve and all of us **both** an immortal spirit and a human body.

Maybe we should be called "anigels"... or "angimals"!

We "em-body" the spiritual, as Saint John Paul says. The human body can be seen; it is visible. It makes visible the human spirit: soul, mind, and heart—all gifts from God. The only way our spiritual gifts can be made known is through our bodies.

In other words, the body is like a sacrament!

Bodies vs. Avatars

When you play a video or board game, you have a figure that represents you to move around in the game. This is called an *avatar*, and you control it.

But this is NOT you. It's not a real body, and it has no spirit. It does not actually breathe, eat, or become tired. An avatar has no feelings and cannot love. It's not a whole person but an empty shape that helps your imagination.

An avatar's figure is only a **symbol.** It isn't you, but just represents you. If the avatar looks dead on the screen, it's not really dead, and you're not really dead, since the avatar only represents you.

Not so with your body! The bodies God gave us are not avatars; they are not symbols. Our bodies are complete and reveal that we are whole people. We should never view our real bodies as meaningless avatars. Our bodies matter! Matter matters! Our spirits are complex, important, and united with the body.

Absent Avatar or Present Person?

When you are present, your whole self is present, visible and invisible. Not just your body. Not just your spirit. YOU are present!

Whenever we meet another person, we are not meeting an empty shape. A *whole* person meets another *whole* person. We know this because we understand the body as "sacrament." This is why it is important to treat other bodies with respect, not as if they were avatars or symbols.

This is why we give others our full attention when we are together and leave our electronic devices off. We make eye contact with them. This is how whole people relate to each other in a healthy way with their bodies.

24

To Know and Be Known

Our bodies bring about the hidden realities of all of us. You can *know* others through their bodies.

For example, when you see a toddler girl, you can know certain things about her. You know that she is very young, that she is learning to walk and talk, and that she needs others to take good care of her. You know this by her body.

When your little brother is crying, you know that something is wrong. His body tells you that he is unhappy. A crying avatar is not really unhappy, but your little brother really is.

When your grandma blows you kisses as you drive off, you know she loves you. Her body shows you this.

You can **be known** by others through your body. When people see you, they know that you are a growing, school-aged child. They know whether you are a girl or a boy. Your body makes that known.

When you raise your hand in class, your teacher knows you want to say something. Your body told her that.

When you hug your parents, your body shows your love for them. They know your love through your body. Your body is a visible sign that brings about an invisible reality.

Wholly Holy

When we view the body as a sacrament, we see that the body is sacred because it is you. Sacraments are sacred because God works through them. Since your body is like a sacrament, let God live in you deeply — and act through you.

Then you will be wholly holy!

"In human life, signs and symbols occupy an important place. As a being at once body and spirit, man expresses and perceives spiritual realities through physical signs and symbols."

CCC 1146

Mission: Remind yourself that you are a whole person and that what you do with your body matters. Smile at the people you meet today and make that smile a blessing by praying silently, "God bless you."

3 The Only Response Is Love

Seeing with "Son-glasses"

How many people do you see every day? When we meet another person, we see his or her body, but remember that each body presents realities that lie hidden.

Each time we encounter another person, we need to use our sacramental "Son-glasses." There is more to that person than meets the eye. We need to be aware of the whole person: body and spirit.

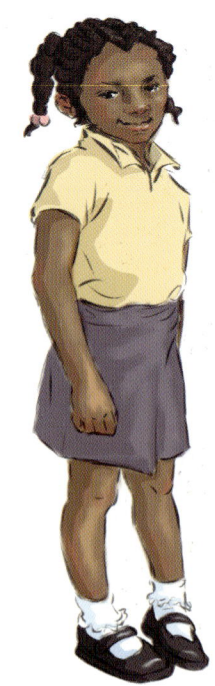

My classmate, Maya, is like a sister to me. I can see she's made in God's image.

When two people meet, it is a meeting of two bodies. And it is more. It is a whole person meeting a whole person. And how should whole people treat each other? Jesus says, "Love your neighbor as yourself." He also tells us, "Love one another as I have loved you." And Jesus loves us to death. Literally! Once we understand the body as the visible sign of a whole person, we then see people properly and respond with love. Jesus shows us that love is the only proper response to another person.

We show love to our Creator by loving His creation. The pinnacle of His creation is the human person, made in His image and likeness. Because of this, showing love to others is a way to love God.

Do you feel deep amazement when you look around at your classmates? God is so creative and good!

We are like snowflakes; each one of us is unique. No two people are alike. God plans each of us and loves us into existence. Each person, each body has his or her own strengths, talents, interests, and gifts.

Do you feel deep amazement when you see a tiny baby? Or a very elderly lady? Or a strong, young athlete? All have worth and dignity, and all are amazing.

Remember what we learned about avatars in the last lesson? Our own bodies are not avatars, and other people's bodies are not avatars either. The people around us (whose bodies we see) are far more important and precious than other things in life, like toys, games, TV, food, etc....

When we see the body as a sacrament, then we know that we are to respond with love. People deserve love.

The chart to the right shows the differences between a person and a thing.

How Do You Approach People & Things?

Person	Thing
Is to be loved	May be used
Is to be respected	Can be controlled
Makes his or her own choices	Has no choice
Is free	Has no freedom
Is mysterious	Can be labeled
Has feelings	Has no feelings

Serving with Love

There are many ways to treat others with love. Love means making a gift of myself to others and receiving their gifts. We can do this by serving others, thanks to our bodies. For example, your parents serve you by taking care of you, and you serve them with obedience and love. Your teachers serve you by giving you an education, and you serve them by obeying and learning from them.

Neighbors serve each other with friendliness and small favors; friends serve each other by talking and playing together.

My brain is a gift. I'll do my best to receive an education.

My arms are strong. I can help Mr. Greenleaf.

Using Is Not Love

But remember, each person is more important than any service he or she can provide, because people are not things.

We must never look at someone in terms of what we can get out of them. Many think the opposite of love is hatred. But the opposite of love is using people. Using people only to "get stuff" is not love; it is greed. When we do that, we treat a person like a thing. People are more important than things!

Love means giving the gift of ourselves **to** others. Love is also receiving the gift of self **from** others. Giving and receiving are necessary to love. Using is not loving.

Before anything else, we must see and appreciate the wholeness of all persons. Any services they may offer are secondary.

33

Use or Love?

Look at this picture. Which word-bubble shows a loving response to the body, the whole person?

On the top the daughter uses flattery and empty promises to get her mother to do what she wants.

On the bottom the daughter is being honest and true to her mother, speaking politely and not trying to control her. The way she asks shows that she knows her mom has freedom to say yes or no.

34

What a neat toy! That boy likes the same things I do! Maybe we can be friends!

What a neat toy! How can I get it from that boy?

Look at this picture. Which one of the boy's thoughts reflects that people are more important than things?

The thoughts *on the left* show that the boy sees the other child as a whole person and responds in a loving way, putting the person above the toy.

The thoughts *on the right* show that the boy values a toy—a thing—above the person holding it. He wants to **use** the person to get the toy. He is seeing the body as an object; he is not seeing in a sacramental way.

Body + Spirit = Whole Person

Our own bodies need a loving response too, even from ourselves! What we do with our bodies, we do as **whole** persons. If a boy steals a cookie, his whole self has stolen the cookie, not just his body. If a girl tells a lie, her whole self has told a lie, not just her body. In the same way, if a child writes a card for a sick friend, the whole child shows kindness. That child respects his or her own body.

Both the body (visible) and the spirit (invisible) are important. Some people think they only need to pray or study with no exercise, for example. They focus too much on the spirit, and they forget about the body. God wants us to cherish our bodies.

Other people may think only about their bodies—the food they eat, the sports they play, their hairstyles and clothes—and they forget to read good books or pray.

God wants us to cherish our souls, minds, and hearts too. The body and spirit are precious gifts from Him.

If we properly understand the human body, we will want to love. We love others and we love ourselves because we understand that the body makes visible our hidden self.

If we could actually see God living within our neighbors and ourselves, we would be overwhelmed with joy! We can't see that here on earth, but we can know it to be true. One day in heaven, we will be eternally amazed at each other and ourselves — body and spirit!

"By charity, we love God above all things and our neighbor as ourselves for love of God."   *CCC 1844*

Mission: Choose one way to serve someone with your body today. Try to take a day off from technology and focus on a body-to-body encounter. You can set the table for your parents, pull weeds for your neighbor, help someone carry heavy bags or school books, or just play with someone who is standing alone. How can you respond to another's body with love?

4 How Does This Fit in Holy Writ?

The Body and Our Faith

Did you know that there is a different way of answering the most basic questions of our faith? It's one that you might be surprised to learn. So many important things on earth begin with the **body:**

Where did Christianity begin? *In a BODY!*

Whose body? *Mary's BODY!*

What is the center of Christianity? *A BODY!*

Whose body? *Christ's BODY!*

How are the bodies of Jesus and Mary like sacraments? Thinking about this will help us to understand our own bodies as sacraments.

38

Mary's Body

Mary was born, like all of us, with a body and soul. She had a little girl's body that grew in time into a woman's body. She walked and talked, played and learned, ate and slept like all of us.

Imagine when the angel Gabriel appeared to Mary. He delivered the amazing message from God the Father that she would become the mother of the Messiah!

In other words, God was asking her,
"Will you give My Son a body?"
"Will you be the Mother of God?"

Mary's *Fiat* ("Let it be done") brought about the Incarnation, or the "em-body-ment" of God the Son. He became a little baby in her womb. Mary said "yes" to God with her whole self — body and spirit. From then on, her body revealed her as the Mother of God. Her body was a very special "sacrament," like a sacred tabernacle.

What does the tabernacle look like in your church? It's usually a beautiful golden box, like a treasure chest, where we keep our most precious treasure, Jesus' Body in the Eucharist.

Mary's body was a living tabernacle when she was carrying Jesus' Body in her womb. Her body hid Christ Himself, and she brought Christ to others wherever she went. Her body was the home of the King!

By receiving Communion, we can be like Mary: our body encounters Christ's Body!

**The tabernacle hides
the Body of Christ**

Like all of us, Mary was surrounded by others in her family and community, and she treated their bodies with love.

She also gave her own body in love and service to others. When she learned that Elizabeth, her older cousin, was pregnant, Mary immediately made the journey to visit Elizabeth and her unborn baby during this special time. Mary stayed with Elizabeth for three months, giving the gift of her time and her company.

So be imitators of God, as beloved children, and live in love, as Christ loved us and handed himself over for us as a sacrificial offering to God for a fragrant aroma. *Eph. 5:1-2*

**Mary's body hid
the Body of Christ**

41

Our Lady loved Jesus and took care of him with her body as all mothers do. She washed Him, fed Him, taught Him, and rocked Him to sleep. Later, at the most important moment of His life (and of human history), she stood, with her body, at the foot of His cross, loving Him through His Passion and suffering with Him.

Mary responds to all of us with love. At the Wedding Feast in Cana, Mary was the one to notice that the wine was running out. She did not hesitate or ignore the problem. Her eyes saw the problem, her feet took her to Jesus, and her voice petitioned Him. In her love and concern for the young married couple, she went to Jesus to ask Him for His help. In the same way, she intercedes for all of us. In heaven, Mary now brings our prayers before her Son, Jesus.

Jesus' Body

Jesus, more than anyone, knows the body as sacrament. His Body is the ultimate sign of God. He is God. He is a living sacrament.

The human body has always been holy, but from the moment of His Incarnation, Jesus, the Son of God, became a human like us and gave the body an even higher meaning.

"Through the fact that the Word of God became flesh, the body entered theology… through the main door." *Theology of the Body 23:4*

43

Our Lord is fully human as well as fully God.
When He was born long ago in Bethlehem, Jesus
had the body of a little baby. He knows what it
is to be em-bodied. He walked through dusty
streets and worked in the hot sun. He ate fish
and bread, and needed water when He was
thirsty. He laughed with friends and wept when
His loved ones died.

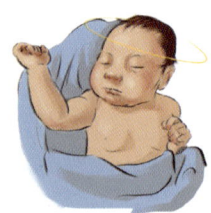

Christ's body revealed His hidden Self as He healed the sick and forgave sinners. When He walked on water, His body showed that He is divine. When He raised Lazarus from the dead, Jesus gave us a glimpse of His plan to save us and conquer death.

Jesus shows us how to treat other bodies with love. During His life on earth, He taught us, healed us, and forgave our sins. But we can best understand His love for us when we see Our Lord hanging on the cross. He offered His Body, His whole Self, to save each of us. He makes Himself a Gift.

The body is so important that Jesus gives us His own Body as a sacred, precious Gift in the Eucharist. At the Last Supper, Jesus said the most important words of the universe:

"This is my Body."

Then He continues:

"... given up for you."

In other words, Jesus tells us what the body is made for: **Love.**

Let us say with Jesus and Mary, "This is my body—my body as a sacrament—given up for you."

"Through Jesus Christ the invisible God becomes visible. He becomes a man like us."
YOUCAT 9

The Feast of Corpus Christi

The body is central to our faith, so, of course, the Body of Christ is highly venerated by Catholics. We enjoy a special feast day called Corpus Christi (Body of Christ) to celebrate the wonder and joy of Christ's Body in the Eucharist. It usually falls in June, a few weeks after Easter.

Many parishes celebrate with Mass, followed by a procession (like a big parade), with the Eucharist displayed in a monstrance for all to see.

This feast day was inspired by St. Juliana's visions from God. It was first celebrated in Liége, France, in 1246 and is now observed worldwide.